Remembering Michael

A STORY ABOUT A FAMILY
WHERE A BABY BROTHER DIES AT BIRTH

Anita Harper
Illustrated by Helen Averley

SANDS

STILLBIRTH AND NEONATAL DEATH SOCIETY

This book has been made possible by **BBC Children in Need** and **Glaxo Holdings plc**.

SANDS also wishes to thank

Ajahma Charitable Trust
AMEC plc
Ayrshire SANDS
Boots Charitable Trust
Four Oaks Infant School, Sutton Coldfield
High Wycombe SANDS
Playtime Day Nursery, Sutton Coldfield
Royston SANDS
Shropshire SANDS
Surrey SANDS
Test Valley School, Stockbridge

and the many other members, friends and supporters of SANDS who have contributed in whatever way to the publication of this book.

This book is for all the children who have had a baby sister or brother who died. You may feel that you are the only person who has had this experience, but you are not. What happens to the people in the story may be like what happened in your family, or it may be quite different. I hope that reading it will make it easier for you to tell people what it was like for you.

It was one of those days in the Lewis family. Sally was making cakes out of flour and sand and plasticine. David was reorganising his room for the fourth time that day. Mum was so pregnant she could hardly move.

And then it started. Mum gave a groan and screwed up her face. Dad rushed in. The baby was going to be born soon.

"David, run next door."

David's heart was beating fast as he knocked at the flat next door. Mrs Patel knew why he had come.

"Mum's started having the baby."

"Right," smiled Mrs Patel. "You go and get that sister of yours."

"And bring your draughts set," called Mr Patel from inside.

It was getting late. David had won seven games of draughts and Mr Patel had won six. Sally was asking Mrs Patel to read her Cinderella for the fifth time.

"Do you think Mum's all right?" asked David.

"Oh, I expect so," said Mrs Patel. "Having a baby can take a while, you know."

Just then the telephone rang. Mr Patel answered it.

"Your dad is on his way home from the hospital," he told them, putting the phone down.

"Is it a baby girl?" Sally was pulling at his jacket.

"Your Dad wants to tell you all about it himself," said Mr Patel, picking her up.

David felt uncomfortable. Mr Patel didn't look very happy.

It was long past their bedtimes when Dad got back. He sat down on the settee with them. Sally climbed on to his lap.

"When can we see the baby, Daddy?"

"I'm afraid I have some bad news for you," said Dad. "Something went wrong when the baby was in Mummy's tummy. Our baby was born – dead."

He started crying.

"Why did the baby die?" David asked.

"We don't know," said Dad. "Nobody knows. He's a little boy and he looks perfect."

"I don't want him to die." Sally was crying too.

David tried to understand, but it didn't make sense. Old people die or soldiers fighting in wars, but not babies, not unless they are starving to death or have some awful diseas

"Couldn't the doctors do anything to help him live?"

"No," said Dad. "There was nothing they could do."

"It's not fair!" said Sally.

"I know," said Dad. "I know."

In the morning, Dad was busy phoning people.

"I don't want to go to school," complained Sally. "I want to see Mummy."

David didn't feel much like going to school either. People might ask if the baby had been born yet. He didn't know what he would tell them.

Dad agreed that they could both stay off school. He said he would telephone their teachers, and explain what had happened.

David went up to his room and stared out of the window. Why did this have to happen to his family? He kicked a toy car across the room. Then Dad called him from downstairs.

"I want to see Mummy! I want to see Mummy!" Sally was jumping up and down on the settee. David wanted to see her too. He wanted to make sure she was all right.

The hospital had long corridors and a strange smell. Mum was sitting up in bed with her best nightdress on. She reached out her arms when they came in and hugged them all. "How are you?" asked Dad, squeezing Mum's hand.

"Tired," said Mum. "It was hard to sleep."

Sally had got off the bed. She was opening all the cupboards. "Where's the baby?"

There was silence for a moment, then Mum said, "He's in a room downstairs."

"I want to see him," said Sally. The nurse came in.

"I could bring him up, if you like," she said.

"What about you, David? Would you like to see him?"

David wasn't sure. "What will he be like?"

"Well," said Mum, "he's about this big." She held out her hands. "And he's got a lots of black hair."

David decided that if he didn't see the baby, he would always wonder what he was like.

The nurse put the baby gently into Mum's arms. He was wrapped in a shawl. Mum's eyes filled with tears.

"He's so beautiful," she said, stroking his cheek.

Sally climbed up on to the bed. "Can I hold him?"

"Yes, if you're careful."

David moved a little closer. He could see the black hair and a wrinkled and blueish face. His eyes were closed, but it was clear that he was dead and not sleeping.

"I think he looks a little bit like you, David," said Mum. She put the baby in his arms. He was cold and stiff.

"Hello, little brother," he whispered in his ear.

"I'll take a photograph of you holding him." The nurse had a camera. It seemed a funny idea.

"What shall we call him?" said Sally. They all looked hard at the baby, trying to imagine what name would suit him.

"I'd like to call him Michael," said Mum.

"I'll always remember you, Michael," said Dad, tearfully.

A doctor came in to see how Mum was.

"Why did our baby die?" Sally asked him straight out.

"We don't know," said the doctor. "Sometimes it happens."

That night in bed, David heard Sally crying in the next room. Dad was on the telephone downstairs. David went into her room. Sally was curled up with her thumb in her mouth, sobbing.

"What's the matter?" asked David.

"I wanted Mummy to play with me in the park, but she couldn't because of the baby. I hated the baby then and I wished it would go away. And now it has." David didn't know what to say. He didn't think you could kill people by thinking bad things about them, but everything was so upside-down at the moment, it was hard to know what was true.

Just then the doorbell rang. It was Auntie Jean, Mum's sister. She was one of David's favourite people.

"Auntie Jean!"

"I'll be up in a minute. Just let me take my coat off and say hello to your dad." It seemed ages before Auntie Jean stopped talking to Dad and came upstairs.

"So you went to see your baby brother today," she said, hugging them both.

"Yes, but he's dead and I made him dead," said Sally, "because sometimes I didn't want him to be born. I didn't want Mummy looking after a baby all the time and forgetting about me." Auntie Jean looked serious and sad.

"Oh, sweetheart, the baby didn't die because of what you

thought. It's not anybody's fault that he died. You know, I was about the same age as you when your mum was born. I can still remember how jealous I felt every time your gran picked her up. I was really glad she was there to play with when she got bigger, but I didn't feel that in the beginning." Sally listened wide-eyed.

"What about you, David?" Auntie Jean turned to him.

"I wasn't too keen on having another sister, I think one's enough. But a brother would be different." Auntie Jean nodded. Sally was falling asleep.

"Will you stay, Auntie Jean?"

"I can stay until the end of the week," she said. "But I'm going to sleep now, and so are you."

The next day Dad brought Mum home from hospital. She looked very pale. She didn't say much and went straight to bed.

Auntie Jean went to fetch Gran and Grandad Lewis. Dad cooked them fish fingers and baked beans, but no one felt much like eating.

"I want Mummy to be better," said Sally. "I want to show her what I've been making."

"She needs time to rest," said Dad.

Then Gran and Grandad arrived. Suddenly the house was full of people.

"How about a walk to the park, David? Just the two of us," said Grandad.

It was a relief to get out of the house with Grandad. People were washing their cars and taking their dogs for walks.

"Have you heard of a baby dying before?" David asked.

"Well, yes, I have. My mother, that's your great-grandmother, had a baby who died before I was born. But I didn't know about it until years later."

David was quiet. It did happen to other people.

When they got back to the house, Mum and Dad and Gran and Auntie Jean were talking about the funeral.

"It's going to be on Friday," said Dad to Grandad.

"What's a funeral?" asked Sally.

"It's when we say good-bye to the person who has died," said Dad.

"I want to say good-bye to Michael," said Sally. Everyone was suddenly quiet.

"People often get upset at funerals," Mum said at last, "because it's the last time they will be with that person's body."

"Why, what happens to their body then?" David felt glad Sally was asking the questions. Mum sighed.

"We have two choices," she said. "Either we can have Michael's body burnt to ashes and then the ashes can be mixed with the air or with the water in a river or stream, or they can be put into the ground. Or we can put his body in a box and bury it in the ground and he will be part of the earth and help to make other things grow."

"He won't feel any pain," said Dad. "When you die your body doesn't feel things any more."

"I think we should bury his body," said Sally.

"I think so too," said Mum.

"So can we come to the funeral?" David asked.

"I'll think about it," said Dad.

"I'll be good," said Sally. She wasn't going to be left out.

The next day Dad was busy arranging the funeral. He said he had been to see a funeral director called Mr Mathews and had chosen a small white box for Michael to be buried in, and some flowers to put on top of it.

On Friday morning David woke up feeling worried about the funeral. People might get really upset. It could be embarrassing. What if he wanted to leave...?

At that moment Auntie Jean came in.

"How are you this morning?" She looked concerned.

"I'm not sure I want to go to the funeral now." He always felt he could tell Auntie Jean the truth.

"What are you worried about?" She stroked his forehead.

"I'm worried about everybody being upset or acting in funny ways." She looked thoughtful.

"People may be upset. You may feel like crying yourself, but that's all right. Crying can help you to feel better afterwards. Is there anything else?"

"I might want to leave."

"I'll be there. If you want to leave, just nudge me."

David felt better. At least someone was listening to him. It made all the difference.

Breakfast was quiet. Grandad arrived, but Gran was staying at home with a headache. Then it was time to drive to the cemetery. There were big entrance gates and rows and rows of gravestones with the names of people who had been buried there.

Mr Mathews was waiting for them at the gate and so was Mum's friend, Margaret. Mr Mathews got the little white box out of his car. It was hard to think of Michael's body being inside. Mum and Dad held on to each other tightly. Eventually they came to the place where a hole had been dug for the little box. Mr Mathews had brought some straps so he could lower the box down gently.

Margaret read a poem about a flower that grew in the desert and blossomed for just one day every five years. It made everybody cry and look for tissues. David wondered if he should cry, but he didn't feel like it. A robin had come and perched on the pile of earth beside the hole. It seemed to be listening too.

Soon the words were finished and they were all walking back along the path towards the cars.

Back at the house they had tea and sandwiches. Nobody spoke very much and David was glad when Grandad suggested a game. Whatever they played, David always won, but Grandad never seemed to mind. Gradually people got ready to leave. Auntie Jean gave him a piece of paper with her telephone number on it.

"Give me a ring if you feel like a chat," she said, giving him a big hug. David felt grateful. Sally was pulling at her.

"Don't go, Auntie Jean."

"I'd love to stay with you, sweetheart. But I have to go back to work." She picked Sally up and gave her a big kiss. Grandad came and shook David's hand. He slipped a pound coin into it at the same time. It was something that he always did.

David didn't really want to go to school on Monday. Everyone would want to know why he was away last week and he didn't know what to say.

The bell went and he ran into the playground. Everyone was pushing in through the double doors.

After his first lesson Miss Oliver, his form teacher, called him over.

"I was sorry to hear about your baby brother dying. It must be a difficult time for you at home."

"Yes." David nodded. "It is. Everything's in a muddle." Miss Oliver seemed to understand.

Outside in the playground Steven was showing off his new trainers. Then people started discussing a test they had last week. David started feeling left out. He wasn't sure if the others were avoiding him or perhaps they didn't know what to say to him about the baby.

As he was leaving the playground at the end of the afternoon, a boy he hadn't spoken to before came over to him. His name was Winston.

"I heard what happened," he said. "The same thing happened to me last year. My mum had a baby girl, but she only lived for a few weeks. It was really bad not knowing if she was going to live or die. People kept coming round to see how my mum was, but they never asked me. My uncle kept saying: 'You must look after your mum, you know. It's really hard on her.' I could see that, but it was hard on me too."

Winston threw a stone so hard it bounced off the wall. It was obvious he was angry and David could see why.

"I haven't told anyone else – except my dog," said Winston. "I thought you'd know what I mean." David nodded. They walked along the street together and Winston showed David some steps that led down to a canal. They walked a while and threw stones at a floating can.

"I've got to go. See you," Winston said finally. David stayed and watched a stick that was floating in the middle before walking home.

It was a rainy Saturday afternoon. David was bored. Sally was playing with her dolls in the corner of the living room.

"This one is dead," she said, wrapping up her smallest teddy.

"Not all babies die, you know," said Mum, quietly. "We were unlucky."

"I know that," said Sally, "but this one is dead and I'm going to bury it in the ground."

David decided to join in. First he pretended to be the grave digger digging a hole in the ground. Then he pretended to be the funeral director driving to the cemetery with the coffin in the back of his car. Then they both pretended to be doctors in the hospital. They put all the dolls and teddies in a row and pretended they had just been born and some were going to live and some were going to die.

It was a while since Michael's funeral. David decided to go for a walk by the canal. He felt things should be getting back to normal by now, but they weren't. His mum didn't seem like his mum any more. One minute she would be crying and the next she would be angry. Sometimes she just sat staring at nothing for ages. That was the worst.

David felt more and more mixed up. It seemed even worse for Sally. Sometimes she woke up in the night crying. Then Mum or Dad would sit with her until she went back to sleep again.

David threw a last stick in the water and watched it float towards the bridge. Then he started the walk back home.

When David got in, Mum looked frightened and upset.

"Where have you been?" she said. "I was just telephoning John's mum to see if you were there. I've been so worried." Then she burst into tears. Somehow, David thought, all this was to do with Michael dying.

That night David decided to miss supper and he got ready for bed early. He always put himself to bed now. It used to make him feel grown up, but now he wished he could have a cuddle now and then, like Sally, and someone telling him that he was important too. He got his old teddy out of the top cupboard and took it to bed with him. He must remember to put it back in the morning.

David was sitting at his school desk near the window. Today he had an ache in his stomach that wouldn't go away. Suddenly he found himself listening to Miss Oliver.

"Everything is born and everything dies. Look at the rivers. They begin as streams high up in the mountains and they have their life gathering water and travelling through the countryside. What happens to the river at the end of its journey?"

Linda put up her hand. She always knew the answers.

"It goes into the ocean."

"Yes," said Miss Oliver. "It loses its life as a river and it becomes part of the life of the ocean."

David felt his stomach relax. He liked that idea, and he could see that it was true. In fact, when you thought about it, if you just had birth and no death, things would get over-crowded pretty quickly.

The bell rang and everyone started talking and packing up their books. David went over to Miss Oliver's desk.

"It still hurts when someone you love dies," he said.

"I know," she said. "It's sad for those left behind."

David ran across the playground and out through the gates. He could feel the strength in his legs carrying him along and the breath in his lungs. He was alive – maybe not for ever, but for now, and he was going to enjoy it.

David lay in bed watching the shadows. He was thinking about Michael. Downstairs he could hear his parents' voices.

When he was younger, he remembered asking his dad lots of questions and his dad always had an answer. But grown-ups didn't have all the answers about death. It seemed as frightening to most of them as it was for him and Sally. Maybe more so. Miss Oliver had seemed to understand though. He had felt better after talking to her. Then he remembered the piece of paper Auntie Jean had given him. She had told him to telephone her. He took it from his drawer and crept downstairs. The telephone was in the hall. He dialled the number and waited.

"Hello, David." It was so good to hear Auntie Jean's voice again. "How are you?" she asked.

"I'm all right," David replied. "But I'm a bit worried about Mum. It's like she isn't really here any more. She gets my dinner and does the washing and things like that, but I don't think she cares about me any more. I think she's thinking about Michael all the time." He didn't realise how angry and upset he felt about it until he started talking.

"If Michael was here he'd be crying and making messes and causing trouble. Just because he didn't have time to do any of those things, everyone thinks he's perfect." He stopped, wondering if he'd said too much.

"You're right. It's not fair, is it, Love?" Auntie Jean was on his side. He felt relieved. Just then he heard his parents moving their chairs in the kitchen.

"I've got to go. Bye, Auntie Jean." But before he could put the phone down, the kitchen door had opened and Mum was standing there. David expected her to get angry and tell him to go back to bed at once, but she didn't. Instead she sat down next to him on the stairs and put her arm round his shoulders.

"Oh David, I'm sorry I've been in such a state." At last he could feel she was there again, his mum, just like she used to be, caring about him. He buried his head in her chest and held her tight. He was crying and so was she, but it didn't seem to matter.

Gradually things began to get better after that. Mum and Dad seemed to spend more time with David and Sally.

Then there was Michael. He felt like part of the family too, even though he had been with them for such a short time. Sometimes they took flowers to the place where he was buried and sometimes they remembered him at home.

Mum would light a candle by his photograph and get out the book with all the cards and photographs and the little bracelet with his name on from the hospital. They would each say what they remembered about him.

"I remember his wrinkly face," said Sally.

"And I remember how he looked a bit like you, David," said Mum and everyone laughed as David wrinkled up his face.

"And I was afraid to look at him to begin with," he said, remembering.

"I shall always remember Michael," said Dad looking at one of the photographs.

As they talked, it was almost as though Michael was there with them. There was a safe warm feeling in the room. David couldn't remember any times quite like it from before Michael. He breathed a sigh of relief and said a secret "thank you" inside.

Published by SANDS
Stillbirth and Neaonatal Death Society
28 Portland Place
London W1N 4DE
Charity Registration No 299679
Company limited by guarantee no 2212082

First edition 1994
ISBN 1 869903 21 8

Copyright © 1994 SANDS
Text copyright © 1994 Anita Harper
Illustration © 1994 Helen Averley

Design: Krystyna Hewitt

Printed and bound in Singapore